EXPLORER B

WOLVES

D0447656

by
Julia L. Andrews

A TRUMPET CLUB ORIGINAL BOOK

to Peter the Wolf

Published by The Trumpet Club
666 Fifth Avenue, New York, New York 10103

ISBN: 0-440-84302-2

Printed in the United States of America
January 1991

10 9 8 7 6 5 4 3 2 1
CW

PHOTOGRAPH CREDITS

p. 25: © Pat Crowe / Animals Animals. *p. 26:* © David Mech / International Wolf Center. *p. 27: top,* Animals Animals; *bottom,* © Lynn Rogers, 1984. *p. 28: top,* © Lynn Rogers, 1985; *bottom,* © Leonard Lee Rue III / Animals Animals. *p. 29: top,* © Lynn Rogers, 1989; *bottom,* © Charles Palek. *p. 30: top,* © Lynn Rogers, 1986; *bottom,* © Lynn Rogers, 1987. *p. 31: top,* © Lynn Rogers, 1988; *bottom,* © Lynn Rogers, 1988. *p. 32:* © Lynn Rogers, 1984.

Cover: © Lynn Rogers, 1987

Contents

Introduction

Werewolves and Real Wolves

During the 1500s, a small German village was supposedly terrorized by a "werewolf" for 25 years. Sixteen people were killed. A man named Peter Stubbs was finally accused of the crimes. During his trial, he claimed that he could turn into a wolf by wearing a magic wolfskin belt given to him by the Devil. The villagers thought Stubbs was a werewolf.

But Stubbs wasn't really a werewolf—he was a murderer. For centuries, though, people believed that all wolves were evil. Today, we know that werewolves exist only in horror movies. And people are beginning to understand and appreciate real wolves at last.

What changed people's negative attitudes toward real wolves? Scientific research. Up until recently, people knew very little about wolves. Then wildlife biologist Adolph Murie devoted his entire life to these mysterious animals. In the 1930s, Murie followed wolf packs in Alaska to learn as much as he could about them. Through careful observation and research, he found that wolves were intelligent, affectionate animals.

Murie's discovery made many scientists curious to find out more facts. There was one problem, though. Most wolves live in remote, northern places and have learned to avoid humans. This makes it difficult for us to observe them. However, with the help of modern technology, scientists have solved this problem.

For 7 weeks every winter, Dr. Rolf Peterson flies in a tiny plane over Michigan's Isle Royale National Park, an island in Lake Superior. He wears a big set of headphones and listens for loud radio beeps. Peterson is tracking the wolves of Isle Royale.

Some of the wolves on the island wear collars equipped with radio transmitters that constantly send out signals. (During the summer, Dr. Peterson captures and collars the animals. Then he releases them.) Each wolf has its own signal. Peterson picks up the signals with a radio receiver in the plane. When a signal is loud and clear, he knows which wolf is on the ground below the plane. Tracking the wolves by radio lets him follow the animals' movements without disturbing them. He learns where each pack's territory and hunting trails are located. He also learns how the different packs interact with each other.

Radio collars are great research tools. However, they don't let scientists see firsthand how wolves behave. How do they hunt? How do they raise their young? How do they care for one another? To answer these questions, scientists must live with the wolves.

Some wolf experts raise wolf pups in huge fenced-in areas in the countryside. As the wolves grow up and form packs, the scientists have a chance to observe the wolves' daily lifestyle. But do captive wolves behave the same as wild wolves? To find out, scientists had to study wolves in the wild. Scientist David Mech and photographer Jim Brandenburg went to live with a pack of wild wolves near the North Pole.

Mech is a famous wolf expert who, like Adolph Murie, has spent his life studying wolves. Brandenburg has been fascinated with wolves since he was a boy growing up in Minnesota. Neither man had ever been able to study wild wolves up close. That's why they went to Ellesmere Island in northern Canada. Ellesmere Island is a rocky, icy plain with few trees—a good place to watch wolves.

The men didn't use collars or planes to conduct their research. To follow the animals on their long treks, the two researchers used all-terrain vehicles. And they took with them cameras, pens and paper, warm clothes, and plenty of patience. For three often freezing summers, Mech and Brandenburg pitched their tent near a wolf den. They got an insider's view of wolves in their natural habitat.

Wolves have always been a mystery to humans. But now, people are learning more and more about these mythic animals. So take a seat and get ready for a guided tour of wolf country!

1

What Is a Wolf?

What would have happened if Little Red Riding Hood had met the Big, Bad Wolf and he had invited her to meet his family? She would have been very surprised!

Real wolves are very different from the monsters of fairy tales and folklore. They aren't bloodthirsty or evil. They're caring and affectionate animals.

A wolf is a mammal, just as you are. That means it has hair and a backbone. A wolf is warm-blooded and nurses on its mother's milk. Wolves are *carnivores,* which means they're meat-eaters. (Most of us are *omnivores,* which means we eat meat *and* plants. *Herbivores* are animals that eat only plants.)

To find out what a wolf is, take a good look at another mammal—a pet dog. Dogs can tell you a lot about wolves. Wolves are the ancestors of every pet dog in the world, from tiny poodles to gigantic Great Danes.

Zoologist Desmond Morris thinks that today's dogs made their first appearance when early human societies began to form. Morris believes that cave families sometimes ate wolf pups. Pups that weren't eaten became pets. Trained to help humans, these wolves evolved into pet dogs.

Wolves and dogs belong to a group of carnivorous mammals called *canines*. Coyotes and foxes are also canines. Sometimes it's hard to tell different canines apart. To tell a wolf from a coyote, for example, just compare sizes: Wolves are about twice as big as coyotes. To tell a wolf from a big dog, such as a German shepherd or a husky, compare their tracks and their tails: A wolf walks in a straight line, while a dog zigzags slightly when it walks. A wolf's tail usually hangs straight down; a dog's tail usually sticks up in the air.

Ancient Hunters

Wolf packs have hunted, howled, and roamed the Earth for nearly 2 million years. (Humans have existed for about 50,000 years.) The first wolves probably slept in trees the way leopards do today. Once, hundreds of thousands of wolves lived in most of the forests and plains of the Northern Hemisphere (the part of the world north of the Equator). No other land mammal has ever had such a huge territorial range. In North America, wolves lived anywhere from Mexico City to Greenland, only 400 miles from the North Pole. Now, few wolves live south of Canada.

The two species of wolves in North America today are the gray wolf and the red wolf. The arctic wolf, a type of gray wolf, is found in the icy regions of the continent. The gray wolf lives in the forests of Alaska, Canada, and in parts of the northern Midwest. Because it lives near timber, the gray wolf is also called the timber wolf. Its fur can be gray, black, tan, or black and tan.

The arctic wolf lives on the tundra, or frozen plains, near the Arctic Circle. Its fur is much lighter and thicker than that of the gray wolf. It needs super-thick fur to survive deadly cold Arctic winters.

Despite their name, red wolves come in a variety of colors—red, black, and gray. They're a separate species from gray and arctic wolves. The red wolf once lived in Texas and Louisiana. It is now extinct in the wild. Today, a few red wolves survive in captivity in nature refuges.

North America isn't the only place that wolves now inhabit. They live in parts of Europe and Asia, too. These wolves look very similar to their American relatives, but sometimes they act very differently. The Chinese wolf is a loner. And the Iranian wolf hardly howls at all!

Born To Run

Wolves can run up to 35 miles an hour for short dashes—that's like running 10 blocks in 100 seconds. With their long legs, they can easily follow prey at a trot for hours at a time. It's not unusual for wolves to jog over 40 miles in a single day in search of a moose meal. Wolves have a bend in their legs at the place where a human knee would be. That bend isn't a knee, however. It's the animal's heel! Like all canines, wolves walk on their tiptoes, allowing them to run quickly, quietly, and gracefully.

In wintertime, wolves must trudge through deep snow when they're on a hunt. Their big paws work like snowshoes. A wolf's toes spread out when they touch the snowy ground and keep the animal from sinking.

Thick pads on their paws protect their feet from frostbite. Cherokee Indians appreciated this fact. Before leaving on long winter hunts, they would rub ash on their feet and perform a wolf dance. They hoped to make their feet as "frost free" as wolves' feet.

A Coat for Any Season

Wolves actually have *two* fur coats. The fur you see is made of long, stiff guard (or outer) hairs. Beneath these hairs is a thick, soft coat of underfur. When a wolf swims, its underfur doesn't get wet because its guard hairs are so thick. Wrapped in their thick fur, wolves sleep comfortably in temperatures as cold as 40 degrees (F) below zero!

What Big Teeth You Have, Grandma

Wolves *do* have big teeth. Their four fangs measure 2¼ inches from tip to root. All canines have these distinctive fangs, which is why they're called canine teeth. (You've got canine teeth, too.)

Wolves and all other canines have 42 teeth (humans have only 32). If you looked inside the mouth of a wolf, dog, or human, you'd see four types of teeth—incisors, canines, premolars, and molars. Incisors, in the front, are the slicers that cut into tough flesh. Canines, on the side, are the grabbers. A wolf digs these fangs into prey and hangs on until the victim stops struggling. In the back of the mouth are the premolars and molars. These teeth are the super-crushers. They make food easier to digest.

Why, Grandmother, What a Long Nose You Have!

A wolf snout has to be big enough to hold 200 million smelling cells. A wolf can detect friend, foe, or food from 1½ miles away. Some people believe that a wolf's sense of smell is a million times better than a person's. If your nose worked as well as a wolf's, you could smell a cake baking from 1 mile away.

A wolf has ears that are sharp enough to hear a howl from several miles away. A wolf tunes into the direction of a sound by pricking up its ears and twitching them around. Wolves and dogs can also hear very high sounds that humans can't hear. Blow a dog whistle, and you won't hear a thing. However, a wolf would hear the high-pitched whistle loud and clear.

2

Pack Life:
Top Dogs and Baby-sitters

A pack is a big wolf family—every member is related. Mom, Dad, brothers, sisters, aunts, and uncles all eat, sleep, hunt, howl, swim, fish, play, run, travel, and fight together for most of their lives. An unrelated wolf can join a pack, but only if family members approve. Most wolves belong to a pack. It's the key to their survival. Packs range in size from two to twenty wolves, but the average is about seven members.

David Mech and Jim Brandenburg spent their time on Ellesmere Island with a pack of seven adults and six pups. The men gave the wolves nicknames that suited each animal's personality. They called the male leader of the pack Buster. Every time Buster returned from his travels, the other wolves in the pack gathered around him. They licked his mouth and nudged his neck. Buster accepted—and expected—all this attention. Buster was top dog.

Top dog sounds like a great job, but it's a tough

one. Buster and his mate, Mid-Back, the female top dog, were in charge of the wolf pack. That means feeding many hungry mouths, keeping the animals safe from harm, and generally taking care of the entire family.

Packs of arctic wolves in Alaska and northern Canada can have territories as big as 1,000 square miles. Why do they need so much room? Because food is scarce. The wolves have to travel great distances to find enough prey to feed the pack. The packs of gray wolves that live in Minnesota and Wisconsin roam through forests where plenty of moose, deer, and other prey live. Their territories are much smaller because they don't have to go as far to find food. Even so, gray wolves may have to travel as far as 50 miles a day to get food!

We Are Family

Wildlife writer Barry Lopez was working on a book about wolves. He went to Alaska to do some wolf research. One day, he discovered an old female in a dense forest. She was fat and healthy, even though it was the time of year when food was very scarce. Lopez gave the animal a drug to make her sleep so he could get a closer look at her. He opened her mouth to look at her teeth. Her fangs were ground down to nubs! A wolf with nubs for teeth can't hunt. And an animal that can't hunt doesn't eat. Lopez figured out that the pack made sure she didn't starve. They must have shared their meat with her.

Jim Wuepper, a wildlife photographer, raised a pack of wolves in an enclosed area behind his farm in Michigan. When three pups in the pack died, the adult wolves whined constantly near the pups' den. Wuepper knew that one last pup was still alive. He decided to remove it from the den to make sure it wouldn't die.

The pack was frantic. They searched everywhere for the pup. They whined even more. Wuepper felt that the pack was grieving much like humans in mourning.

Wolves are affectionate animals. They feel a strong family bond. Wolves constantly nudge and lick each other's snouts. These licks are wolf kisses! Wolves aren't shy about showing their affections. They're always snuggling, nuzzling, or tumbling around together. Physical contact keeps the pack together.

Wolves can be pretty silly. When they're not hunting or napping, they chase each other and play tag or hide-and-seek. If there's a stick or piece of hide lying around, they'll play tug-of-war. It's not just the pups that fool around. Grown-ups love to play, too!

Sometimes the pack has unusual playmates—ravens. These big, black birds scavenge dead animals for their food. They follow the wolves on hunts and eat the leftovers. The ravens also eat the wolves' scats, or droppings. Although wolves eat birds, they won't harm ravens. Instead, wolves and ravens play games together. The ravens fly close to a sleeping wolf's head and make a loud racket. If the wolf doesn't budge, the bird buzzes down and caws again until the wolf tries to chase it away.

First Mates

Male wolf meets female wolf. They court each other and become mates. A new pack is formed! When a wolf selects a mate, it stays with that mate for many years. Most other animals breed, then quickly go their separate ways.

Think of how your own family works, and you'll get a good idea of what goes on in a wolf pack. The top dogs in your family may be your parents or grandparents. They make sure you've got food, clothes, and a safe place to live. They hug and kiss you because they love you. They punish you when you misbehave. They make rules so you'll learn to take care of yourself and others.

A wolf pack works the same way. Every pack has a pair of top dogs like Buster and Mid-Back. Since these wolves are the Number One wolves in the pack, scientists call them the *Alpha* male and female. (Alpha, the first letter in the Greek alphabet, means "first.") The Alpha pair are the parents of the pack.

The Alpha male and female don't have equal power. One is usually the leader and the other is second in command. People assume that the male is always the leader, but this isn't true. Many packs are led by females. They tend to be faster runners and better hunters, which makes them more qualified for the job of top dog.

The leader makes all the big decisions for the pack: which direction to travel when hunting for food, when to rest, when to chase prey, and when to flee from danger. While all pack members watch out for danger, the leader is the main guard. Sometimes other wolves try to invade the pack's territory. The leader decides whether the group should attack or hide. Sometimes hawks try to swoop down and steal a fat wolf pup for supper. The leader makes sure that the pups' den is hidden from hungry birds with killer claws. Adult wolves don't have to worry about that kind of danger. They have no natural enemies, which means no other animal preys on wolves for food. However, one animal can be deadly to wolves. It has two legs and carries a gun. The wolves' deadliest enemy is a human hunter. The leader guards the pack from this intruder.

What are the rewards of being the leader? The leader gets a lot of attention. He also gets first pick of any food the pack finds.

Wolves practice a kind of population control. The only pack members allowed to mate and have pups are the Alpha pair. This way, there won't be too many mouths to feed in an overpopulated pack. Other wolves in the pack will mate and bear young if the Alpha pair is lost or killed. The Alpha pair mate each winter for several years. Sixty-three days later, the female gives birth to a new litter, usually five or six pups. More than half of the pups will die within a year. The survivors will join the pack.

As each new litter grows up, the pups take their place in the pack hierarchy. A litter of pups is like a class of students. Some people run for class president. They like to be in charge. Others prefer to follow the leader. That's what it's like with wolf pups. Aggressive pups constantly play-fight with their brothers and sisters. They like to win. They'll boss the other pups around whenever they have the chance. These animals are dominant wolves. (A pup that is very aggressive and strong has the makings of an Alpha wolf.) Submissive wolves are shy. These pups soon give in to their dominant relatives. The more aggressive the wolf, the higher its rank in the pack.

Team Players, Sitters, and Scapegoats

From top dog to low dog, every wolf has to help out with the pack's daily tasks. Teamwork is the only way the pack can survive. The Alpha pair lay down the team rules. If a wolf doesn't follow the rules, it is kicked off the team.

Every member of the pack helps out with hunting. However, pups aren't much good on a hunt. Just like human babies, pups are helpless and need a lot of care. When the pups are first born, the mother wolf stays by the den with them while the others search for food. After a few weeks, she either leaves the pups to fend for themselves or gets some help from a baby-sitter.

Baby-sitters are young, low-ranking male and female wolves. Although a baby-sitter is one of the most submissive adults in the pack, it has a very important job—watching over the pups. Baby-sitters teach them how to hunt and how to respect their leaders. The Alpha has a tough job being Number One wolf, but think how hard the baby-sitter's job is! Keeping track of rambunctious, hungry, yapping pups is rough work!

Once in a while, a young aggressive wolf refuses to go along with the pack rules. It wants to be the leader of the pack, so it challenges the Alpha leader of its own sex: It acts haughty. It ignores the leader. It flirts with the other Alpha wolf. It picks fights. It tries to prove that it can be a better Alpha wolf. Sometimes the challenger wins and becomes the new leader. But many times the challenger loses. There can only be one pair of top dogs in a wolf pack! The loser may leave. It may go off to live by itself, becoming a lone wolf.

People think lone wolves howl at the moon. Actually, the moon has nothing to do with the howling. The animal is just calling out to other wolves, "Hey, here I am! Anyone out there?" The howler could be a member of the pack who got separated and is trying to locate the others. Or it could be a lone wolf who's . . . lonely! If a wolf of the opposite sex is wandering alone in the same territory, the two may get together. They may form a new pack. At last, the loner finally gets to be an Alpha wolf.

Do you know someone who gets blamed for everything that goes wrong? That person is a scapegoat. Once in a while, wolf packs have scapegoats, too. Scapegoats aren't allowed to sleep with the rest of the pack. They're the last to get food. They're forced to live on the fringe of the pack. Other wolves snap and growl if a scapegoat tries to get too friendly. They are the lowest of the low-ranking wolves.

How does a wolf become a scapegoat? If a wolf was a nasty leader, then loses power, the rest of the pack will mistreat it. The pack keeps the fallen leader in its place.

Are the pack members being mean to the loners and scapegoats? Not really. Everything that goes on in a wolf pack is for the good of the group. Wolves with a mind of their own are dangerous to the survival of a pack, though. The Alpha leader expects the pack to obey when it gives the command to charge at prey or retreat from danger. That's why the leader demands a constant show of respect.

3

Yip, Yap, Yowl, Howl

Ahrrrooo! The eerie sound of the wolf's howl has given people the creeps for centuries. Why do wolves howl? For the same reason people talk—they want to communicate their thoughts and feelings.

Wolves start their day with a family sing-along—the chorus howl. After waking up, one wolf starts to howl, and the others join in. Each wolf throws its head back, points its mouth to the sky, and howls. No two wolves sing on the same note. If a wolf hits the same note as its neighbor, it will change its tune. The chorus howl is more than a wake-up call. It's like a big family hug.

Howling keeps the pack united and is usually started by the leader. Before going off to hunt, the pack sometimes howls. After catching large prey, such as deer, the animals often howl. Wolves get split up from their packs. One wolf will go out on a ridge and howl to get the pack members back together. The howl can be heard from 5 miles away. Wolves also howl a lot in January, during the mating season. By summer, the pups are practicing howling for themselves.

Like people, wolves have different voices from one another. The animals know their pack mates by the sound of their howls. When a pack hears a howl, the wolves know if a pack mate or stranger made the sound. The pack will howl to defend its territory. But packs don't always howl back at strangers. A howl from a big pack of intruding wolves could mean trouble. If the two packs met, there would be a deadly battle. So the smaller pack doesn't howl back.

Wolf packs are fairly quiet during the spring after the pups are born. If they howled, they would give away the location of the pups.

Wolves are famous for their howls, but that's not the only sound they make. They also whine, squeak, growl, and bark. Whines and squeaks are friendly greeting sounds. Wolf mothers frequently whine to their pups in the den as a way of saying, "Don't worry, I'm here." Growls send a very different message. Wolves growl to assert their power when threatened. For example, a wolf will growl if another wolf tries to steal its food. When wolves are surprised near their dens, they'll bark. Barking is a warning cry.

Scent Sense

One dog meets another dog. Instantly, they're sniffing away at each other's rump. What strikes some people as rude behavior is a very important form of canine communication. Wolves, dogs, and all other canines recognize each other by their scent. Each animal has its own unique smell. Underneath a canine's tail is a scent gland loaded with information. Canines sniff the gland to check out the new fellow.

A wolf's urine and scats are loaded with a strong odor from the animal's scent glands. Wolves mark their turf with these wastes. While traveling, wolves urinate on bushes, rock piles, and tree trunks every 2 or 3 minutes. Every member of the pack will mark the same spot, creating a group scent.

Wolves also mark with piles of scats. Dominant wolves will scratch the ground to spread the scats around to make a very visible marking. Wolves also have scented pawprints—the scent comes from sweat in the paws. Just by walking wolves leave their mark.

You could make a map of a pack's territory by tracing all its scent marks. In fact, this is how a pack teaches the pups where the trails are in their territory. The scents keep the pups from getting lost.

One whiff of a scented landmark, and a wolf knows if it's on home or enemy turf. Every wolf knows its own "family" smell. They can tell if the scent came from a male or female. They can tell how long ago the scent was made—scent markings last up to 3 weeks.

•   •   •

Understanding Body Language

The position of the tail, mouth, ears, and even fur helps wolves communicate. Wolves use body language to send messages quickly and quietly to the rest of the pack. A wolf sees a human. It frowns and raises its hackles (the fur on its back). In an instant, the pack knows danger is near.

Wolves show their rank in the group through their postures. As soon as they can waddle around, wolf pups climb on top of each other, trying to force their playmate down to the ground. Scientists call this posture the "riding up" position. The pup who ends up on top is the winner.

Wolves and dogs of all ages "ride up" each other to show who's the top dog—at least for that match! The "standing across" position is another dominant posture. (A dominant wolf stands across the front legs of a wolf that's lying down. Doing this shows the wolf lying down who's more powerful.) Other postures are signs of submission. Remember how Buster, the Alpha wolf, was greeted by his pack mates? With lots of licks and nudges. How do you know when a wolf wants to play? It makes a play-bow! Wolves (and dogs, too) lay their front legs down, stick their rumps in the air, and wag their tails.

Talking Heads and Tails

Look closely at a wolf's face, and you'll notice markings that indicate its eyes, lips, and ears. Dark hairs outline the eyes and ears, while white hairs outline the wolf's black lips. These markings make it easier for others to read any change in expression, which signals a change in mood.

Body language helps keep order within the pack. When a wolf misbehaves, the Alpha leader gives it a stern stare. That look says "Start behaving, or else!" It keeps rebellious wolves in line—lower-ranking wolves cringe at the sight of that stare. If a wolf still acts up, the Alpha growls and bares its teeth. It's ready to fight. Most wolves shape up quickly after that. Wolves and dogs stare at each other only when competing for control. (To prevent a dog fight, don't let dogs stare at each other.)

If you want to know a wolf's mood and status in the pack, don't just look at its face—look at its tail. The tip of a wolf's thick tail is dark, which makes it easier to "read" from a distance. A tail that sticks straight out says "I'm the boss." A tail between the legs is a sign that says "You're the boss."

You can pick out the leaders of the pack by observing how they carry themselves. The Alpha pair walk tall and proud. They look like the top dogs. They're the only ones in the pack who walk with their tails held out—a symbol of dominance and leadership. The others usually keep their tails down. If another member of the pack sticks its tail out, that animal is challenging the Alpha of the same sex. That rebellious tail says, "Hey, hot shot! Who's the boss now?" The Alpha may wrestle with the challenger, forcing it to roll over on its belly with its tail between its legs—the sign of a loser.

21

The scapegoat doesn't want to send out any threatening messages, so it tries to look small and weak. It closes its eyes to narrow slits to avoid staring by mistake. It hunches its back and holds its head to the ground. Its tail is always between its legs.

Want to learn wolf body language? Read the chart below.

MESSAGE	HEAD	TAIL	BODY
"Let's play" (play-bow)	ears stand up mouth grinning	wags	front legs down hind legs up
"Nothing's happening" (relaxed)	ears stand up mouth closed	hangs down	standing or lying
"You're the best!" (wolf greeting)	licks your face	wags	jumps up, tries to place front paws on you
"You're the boss!" (submissive position)	ears flat back eyes closed or looking down mouth closed	between legs	rolls over and shows belly
"Want to fight?" (dominant threat)	ears forward teeth bared growls	stands up	standing

22

What does a wagging tail mean? It means "I'm happy! I'm excited! Let's have fun!" Your dog wags its tail when you come home from school because it's happy to see you. Wolves wag their tails when they're happy to see their pack mates. When dogs or wolves want to play, they wag their tails. They wag their tails when they're excited, too. Just before a big hunt, a pack looks like a furry ball of wagging tails: As the animals huddle together to plan the hunt, their tails whip back and forth in excitement.

Pet dogs "talk" to each other in this body language, too. Next time you want to play catch with your dog, ask it in its own language. Make a play-bow and see what answer you get!

4

A Pup's First Year

On his farm in Michigan, Jim Wuepper knew that the big day was almost here. Denali, the female wolf Jim had raised from a pup, was about to give birth. She was the Alpha female in the pack. For the last few days, the mother-to-be spent all her time in or near the den she and the pack had dug for the new family. Shawano, her mate, brought her many gifts of food. He'd whine at the den's mouth, or opening, to let her know a new gift was there. He'd bury chunks of meat near the den. Denali would need this extra food after the pups were born.

Brigit, another female in the pack, guarded the den. Brigit had always tried to steal Denali's meals —but not this time. Brigit seemed to know that the pregnant wolf needed a lot of food for her babies.

Then one day the whole pack acted very excited. And soon four tiny wolf pups were born!

•   •   •

When one wolf howls, the rest of the pack joins in! No two wolves sing on the same note during a chorus howl.

DOMINANCE HIERARCHY

A wolf pack leader holds its tail straight out. Submissive pack members, such as scapegoats and baby-sitters, keep their tails down.

These two timber wolves are the Alpha male and female, the leaders of the pack.

Wolves devour almost every bit of their prey. Nothing goes to waste.

Newborn wolf pups weigh about as much as a big candy bar— 4 ounces!

Two wolf pups emerge from the underground den where they were born.

A wolf pup learns to howl at an early age.

A timber wolf baby-sitter teaches pups pack rules—how to hunt and how to show respect for their leaders.

Wolves can recognize fellow pack members by sniffing their paw prints.

The Alpha pair leads the pack over familiar trails in the hunt for prey.

A wolf is always on the alert for prey—or for predators!

Wolves are affectionate, caring animals—not the evil monsters of myth and legend!

David Mech fastens a metal tag to a wolf's ear so that the animal can be identified if recaptured. It will help researchers learn how far wolves travel.

A Helpless Heap of Wolf Pups

At birth, a wolf pup is a squeaking, helpless creature no bigger than your hand. It's covered with dark, soft fur. Its eyes are closed shut. Its ears flop down. The pup is blind and deaf, and can barely smell a thing. It can't walk, either. To get around, it crawls on its stomach. A wolf pup weighs about as much as a big candy bar—4 ounces.

When a pup pops out of its mother's body, it's wrapped in a protective bag called the amniotic sac. She opens up the sac with rough licks so the pup can breathe. Then she bites off the umbilical cord attached to the pup's belly button. The wolf, like all mammals, nourishes her pups through this cord while they're still inside her body. The wolf gives the newborn a soft nudge toward her nipples for its first meal. Before the day is over, the pup will be joined by its new brothers and sisters.

Usually there are about five or six pups in a litter. But more than half of the pups born each year die before their first birthday: Some are stillborn; some die of disease (that's how three of Denali's pups died). Others are eaten by bears or wolverines that raid the dens. A pup that makes it to age one is a very strong and lucky animal.

Wolves won't have pups if food has been scarce during the year. Instinctively, the animals know that they won't be able to feed extra mouths in the pack.

•   •   •

Life Underground

Pups spend the first 3 weeks of their lives underground in the dark den they were born in. A wolf den is about 15 feet long, and tall enough for a wolf to stand in. It has a big chamber for the pups. Sometimes there's a separate chamber for the mother. Long tunnels, about 2 feet wide, run from the chambers to the outside. Just as people have front doors and back doors on their houses, wolves have several entrances into their dens. Some of these tunnels are as long as a bus. (Don't ever crawl into a wolf's den! The wolves will be very upset!)

About 3 weeks before the pups are born, the mother chooses a safe, dry spot for her den. She's careful to select a location that's close to the pack's hunting grounds. Otherwise, the pack would have to travel too far for food. If the adults go hungry, the pups go hungry. They could even starve to death.

Building a den is hard work. The wolves dig through the ground for several days to create an underground system of tunnels and chambers. For arctic wolves, that means cutting through several feet of rock-hard permafrost—ground that's always frozen—with their claws.

Wolves don't have to build a new den every time a litter is about to be born. Sometimes they'll take over another animal's abandoned home. With a little enlarging and remodeling, fox dens and beaver lodges make excellent wolf dens. The hollow bottom of a big tree or a secret cave are other good den spots. If a den is built in a safe place, wolves will use it over and over again. Scientists found one den in Canada that wolves had used for over a hundred years!

Wolves like high places near water for their dens. Being up high gives the pack a good view of their territory, which is very important when guarding a den from intruders. Flood control is another reason for a high location. When it rains, the water won't collect in the den and drown the pups. It flows downhill.

While the wolves don't want water *in* the den, they definitely want it nearby. If a lake is close at hand, the mother can get a quick drink without leaving her babies for too long.

The First Three Weeks

Wolf pups spend their first weeks sleeping and eating. Because the pups are so tiny, they have a hard time staying warm. They cry if they're apart—wolf pups don't like to be alone. So they sleep together in a big, cozy pile next to their mother, who's always close by. When they wake up, they drink their mother's milk.

For the first few days of the pups' lives, the mother wolf lies on her side, ready to nurse her babies at any time. If a pup wanders off, Mom picks it up very gently between her teeth and brings it back to her side. This coziness is the beginning of a family bond that will last the wolves a lifetime.

The pups don't have teeth when they're born. They don't need them. Their only food is their mother's rich milk. Wolf milk isn't like the milk you buy at the store. Cow milk and human milk are rich in sugar but low in fat. As a result, calves and human babies become hungry again soon after drinking, but this isn't a problem: Because adult cows and humans eat several times a day, they can produce enough milk to feed their babies often. Wolves, however, can't feed their pups every few hours: The mother may have to leave for an overnight hunt. Or she may not be able to produce enough milk because she hasn't eaten in several days. Wolf milk is very high in fat and protein. The rich, warm milk satisfies the hungry pups for a long time.

After mealtime, the mother rolls each pup onto its back and licks its belly. The pup automatically urinates or defecates. The mother takes care of two tasks with one lick of her tongue: She makes sure that the pup gets rid of body wastes, and she teaches the pup submissive behavior—an important lesson in pack life.

Meet the Family

Pups are the center of the pack's life. Everything the pack does revolves around these helpless creatures. Even before the pups are born, the entire pack helps prepare for the new arrivals. Like Brigit and Shawano in Jim Wuepper's pack, the wolves do what they can to make sure the mother and pups have enough food and are safe from harm. To feed the rapidly growing creatures, the pack goes out every night in search of food. The mother stays at home to watch over her brood. The Alpha male (the pups' father) helps out with den duty when he returns from a hunt. He'll crawl into the dark chamber and give the pups gentle nudges or a bath with his tongue.

By the time the pups are 3 weeks old, they open their eyes and see for the first time. Their world looks like a fuzzy blur. In a few weeks, though, they are able to see more clearly. Their floppy ears start to perk up. Now the pups can hear each other! Their stubby legs become strong enough to hold them up. Needle-sharp milk, or baby, teeth poke through their gums. Soon they'll be able to eat meat, although they won't get adult teeth until they're 6 months old.

Now it's time for the pups to leave the den and meet the wolf pack. This is an exciting time for the entire group. Waiting outside the den, the adults pace back and forth. They roughhouse and nuzzle up to each other. They can't wait to see the pups.

The youngsters squeak loudly inside the mouth of the den, then stumble out into the world, where they are greeted with lavish wolf kisses and nudges. No one has to teach the pups what to do—they squeak, kiss, and nudge right back.

Guided by their mother, the pups take short trips outside the den. These trips can be deadly, though. The wolves are constantly on the lookout for hawks and eagles. These birds may swoop down to steal the pups. If a wolf sees one of these birds nearby, it hurries the pups back into the safety of the den.

Food To Go

To get a meal from an adult wolf, all the pups have to do is beg. They mob any adult returning from a hunt with licks, nuzzles, nips, and paws at the big wolf's mouth. Then the adult throws up. It's suppertime for the wolf pups! The pups gobble up every drop.

Eating wolf vomit is probably *not* your idea of a delicious meal. However, that vomit is a rich, nutritious meat stew. The wolf saved that food from its last hunt to give to the pups. Every member of the pack brings the pups food in their stomachs. That's one of the reasons wolves eat so much food at one time. They have to feed themselves *and* the pups. And they need an easy way to carry the food back over long distances. The pack may have a 20-mile hike back to the den.

Raw meat is too hard for pups to chew and digest. But meat that's been sitting in an adult's stomach for a while is just right. That meat is already partially digested, since juices in the wolf's stomach break down, or digest, the meat. If the pups are full of milk when the adults come back from a hunt, the adults bury the vomit in a little hole so the pups can eat it later on. These hiding places for food are called *caches.*

If the pups beg for food when the adults and caches are empty, the pack immediately goes out to hunt.

Wolf School

It's moving day at the den when the pups are about 2 months old. By now, they're the size of very fat cats. They weigh about 15 pounds and are strong enough to live outside of their dens. The pack moves the pups to a new sheltered spot that's closer to the hunting grounds. This spot is called a *rendezvous* site. (Rendezvous means "meeting place.") The pack will leave the pups here and return to them after the hunts. The wolves stay at the sites for a few weeks at a time. The pack moves to a new site when they need to hunt in new areas.

Up until now, the pups have been with their mother almost every minute of the day, but now she needs to join the hunts again to stay healthy. She needs more food than the pack is able to bring back for her. There's only one problem: The pups can't hunt—they're still much too young! Sometimes a mother wolf leaves her pups alone. And sometimes a baby-sitter takes care of the pups. Back at the rendezvous site, the baby-sitter protects, entertains, and teaches the pups while the mother is away.

A baby-sitter teaches the pups the dos and don'ts of pack life. Rule Number One: Respect your elders. The pups in Buster's pack on Ellesmere Island had a baby-sitter named Scruffy, a year-old male.

Scruffy didn't have a high rank in the pack, but as soon as the others went off to hunt, he became top dog. Scruffy was head of the pup pack.

While out on an exploration, Scruffy knocked the pups down and made them cry. He wasn't being a bully. He was teaching them the importance of the pack pecking order—he was the leader and they were the lowly wolves. The pups didn't seem to mind Scruffy's school of hard knocks. They quickly learned to obey and adore their baby-sitter.

A baby-sitter's tough love teaches pups an important lesson of wolf survival—how to respect and obey their leaders. Once, a baby-sitter in Alaska had to leave her pups for a short while. As she trotted off, she heard a rustling sound behind her. One of the pups was tagging along. One stern stare sent the pup back to its brothers and sisters. That stare meant "Go back!" If the pup wandered away from the group, it could've gotten hurt, even killed. By obeying the sitter, the pup stayed out of danger.

Serious Play

When David Mech and Jim Brandenburg came back to their arctic campsite on Ellesmere Island one afternoon, they found streams of toilet paper strung across the whole camp. While the men were off exploring another part of the island, Buster, Mid-Back, and the others had raided the campgrounds.

No matter how old they are, wolves love to play

pranks. They play the same games you play. How about a little leapfrog? Want to play some wolf-tag? Or how about tug-of-war or tumbling?

Eating and playing are the pups' favorite activities—they love to roughhouse all day long. Whatever they find—a feather, a skull, maybe a hide—they turn into a toy. A pup will parade around its brothers and sisters showing off its new prize. Sometimes the pups will fight for these toys, but most of the time fights turn into games.

Wolf play is more than fun and games, though. It's a matter of life and death. These games teach the pups survival skills: They learn to stalk, pounce, swat, and bite. They learn how to hunt and kill.

Young dogs learn the same deadly skills from their games. If you want to see the killer come out in a playful pup, watch how it pounces on some rolled-up socks. Or see how it throttles a ratty old towel. Challenge the puppy to a tug-of-war. Then you'll see how a wolf pup learns to hang on to its prey with its teeth.

One toy that Scruffy's crew loved to play with was an old fox hide. The pups would grab the hide with their teeth and shake it as hard as they could. When wolves catch small prey, they sometimes grab it by the neck and shake it until the neck breaks. The pups' friendly game of shake-the-hide was a lesson in killing.

When the pups are big enough to join the adults on hunts, they test out their new skills—and learn a few more. One of these crucial skills is learning how to howl. Wolf pups have high and squeaky voices at first, but as they grow bigger, they'll soon have a howl that can be heard for miles around.

Family Ties

Even if pups join different packs and live apart, they will always recognize their brothers and sisters. Wolves have excellent memories. By playing, howling, and living together, the pups get to know each other inside out. They develop a strong family bond: They know each other's scent and howl. They can smell the ground and recognize a sister; they can hear a distant howl and recognize a brother. From the moment they're born to the day they die, wolves are very close to their family.

5

The Hunters

It was early winter in northern Minnesota. Deep snow covered the ground. A pack of wolves hadn't eaten in over a week. There was no sign of moose or deer, the animals' favorite prey. Pups constantly nuzzled adults, but got no food from them. The whole pack was hungry.

The wolves spent most of the chilly afternoon napping in a forest clearing. Napping saves energy, an important thing to do when there's no food. Then the Alpha female woke up and stretched her legs. She inhaled the cold air and read the wind. The northeast breeze carried a scent she knew very well —moose!

"Ahrrrooo!" she howled. It was a wake-up call to battle. The other wolves shook off their drowsiness and began to howl, too. The wolves then huddled nose-to-nose in a circle around the Alpha pair. They pointed their snouts in the direction of the moose scent.

In the next 24 hours, the pack traveled 40 miles through snowdrifts, stalked three beasts, fled from human hunters, killed one moose, and ate enough meat to feed about 400 humans.

Hunting is an exhausting, dangerous business for wolves. They don't do it because they're blood-thirsty—they hunt because they're carnivores. If wolves don't hunt, they won't survive.

No TV Dinners

When wolves are hungry, they can't just pop a TV dinner in the microwave oven. Getting a meal takes a lot of hard work.

Wolves spend a third of their lives searching for food. They're nocturnal hunters, which means they usually hunt at night. Wolves, unlike humans, have excellent night vision, as well as a fantastic ability to smell and hear. They see only browns and grays. But in the dark, everything looks dark anyway. Another advantage to hunting at night is that it's easy to hide from prey.

Wolves usually hunt large, hoofed mammals such as moose, elk, deer, sheep, and caribou. An adult male moose can weigh 1,250 pounds and stand 7 feet tall. If a wolf were as big as a moose, it would have a fair chance of winning a fight. However, the largest wolves weigh at most 120 pounds and stand just 3 feet tall. A lone wolf couldn't survive a battle against a hefty moose. This is the reason wolves hunt in packs—they have power in numbers. With dagger-sharp fangs and bone-crushing bites, a pack of wolves is a fearsome enemy for even the largest prey.

Wolves aren't picky eaters. If big prey is scarce, they'll go after smaller game—beavers, hares, even an occasional mouse. Every now and then, wolves go fishing. They'll wade into a stream and lunge at fish. On a good day, they'll trap a fish between their big jaws. But most of the time they end up wet and hungry.

Birds, lizards, snakes, squirrels, grasshoppers, and worms make tasty snacks. Wolves will even gobble up berries, even though they're primarily carnivores.

Wolves can go for 2 weeks without eating. When they *do* eat, though, they eat a lot—it could be a long time before the next meal.

Why wait so long between meals? Because it's so difficult to make a kill. Most large prey such as caribou are hard to catch. They're fast runners that put up a good fight. But that's no problem for the wolf, or is it?

The truth is, wolves *aren't* very successful hunters. For every big beast they kill, fifteen get away. Some outrun the wolves or fight them off. Others may be wounded but still escape. The trick to a successful kill is to go for the weakest prey—the sick, the dying, or the young.

Wolves don't seek out vulnerable creatures to be cruel. Predators simply have better luck hunting weak prey that can't fend off their attackers. Cruelty is a human emotion. Wolves and all other predators just do what comes naturally. In fact, killing weaker members of a herd actually helps the prey. It gets rid of sick animals that could infect the rest of the group, and it also controls the size of the herd, which is important when there's not enough food to go around.

Strategy for Success

What is the wolf's most potent hunting tool? Brain power. Wolves are extremely intelligent animals. Before a pack turns a moose into a meal, the wolves must track down, corner, and capture their prey.

A wolf pack operates like a highly organized army unit when out on a hunt. Using some of the finest ultrasensitive equipment around—their noses, ears, and eyes—the pack identifies and locates the object of its attack. The wolves sniff the wind to figure out where the prey is. The pack is very careful to stay downwind at all times. If the pack moves upwind, the prey might smell the pack and run away.

Their playmates, the ravens, also help wolves locate prey. Ravens can see prey from very far away because they fly high in the sky. The wolves watch where the ravens fly and follow them.

Wolves follow well-traveled routes to find prey. The Alpha pair leads the pack over familiar trails. The wolves know the best way to reach the lake or hill where their prey is likely to gather.

Sometimes wolves take shortcuts. A herd of caribou in Alaska was migrating south for the winter.

They had taken the same route for years. A wolf pack following the herd knew where the caribou were headed—the pack had followed caribou along this route for years. Instead of diligently tracking the herd, the wolves took a shortcut. Two days later they greeted the migrating herd—and attacked.

Imagine running 5 miles an hour all night long. That's how fast wolves travel on their nightly prowls. They can go for 9 hours without stopping. It's no big deal for them to jog 40 miles in a night. If the pack slows down, the Alpha wolf stops the hunt for a few minutes so the wolves can take a quick, refreshing nap. The naps can't be too long, or else the prey will get too much of a lead.

During the winter, when people aren't around, the packs trot along hikers' trails, country roads, and even highways in search of food. The pack makes better time traveling on flat human paths than bushwhacking through deep snow and thick vegetation.

For hours on end, the wolves follow the scents, droppings, and sounds that will lead them to their prey. When the pack actually gets close enough to see the potential victim, the Alpha wolf has to make some big decisions. First, does the pack have a chance of killing this animal? After spending so much time and energy tracking the creature, the pack *needs* food.

Now it's time to map out a stalking strategy: What's the best way to capture this animal? The way wolves hunt deer in a forest is very different from the way they hunt caribou on the plains.

Two factors are important in a pack's hunting strategy: the type of animal being hunted and the lay of the land. Mountain sheep can scramble up a rocky slope in an instant—something wolves aren't built to do. Wolves know this, so they launch their attacks from trails on hills *above* the flock. When the flock runs uphill to safety, the fast sheep easily outrun the wolves. The slow ones are captured by the pack.

What's the best way to catch a caribou? Wolves work as a team to get the job done. Caribou, like musk-oxen and buffalo, travel in herds. When they feel threatened, these animals form a circle to keep wolves out. But a stampeding herd of caribou is a different story. The wolf pack splits up and charges into the cloud of moving prey. Wolves, like pet dogs, love to chase after things that move. Stay still, and they lose interest.

(If you meet a wolf in the woods, don't panic and run. Actually, the wolf will probably be terrified of you and dash off. If it doesn't, move away very slowly.)

Once the wolves have infiltrated the herd, they zero in on the slow-moving animals, usually calves. They isolate a calf and chase it out of the herd, away from its mother's protection.

Relay running is another strategy for hunting caribou. While some pack members rest, others will run after the herd. The resting team takes up the chase if the prey and the hunters pass near them.

Wolves used to hunt antelope on the open range of the Plains states. The wolves didn't chase their prey—the prey actually came to them! The wolves lay down and hid in the tall grasses near a grazing antelope herd. They swished their tails above the grass. Curious antelope (usually the young) wandered over to check out the swishing tails. And then the pack made its move.

No wolves and few antelope roam the Great Plains these days. They were killed off long ago.

Pawnee Indians used the wolves' strategy to hunt antelope and buffalo on the northern Plains. Scouts wore wolf skins and slinked like wolves through the tall grasses as they followed the herds. They were excellent hunters. Because their strategy was so successful, the Pawnee were known as the Wolf People.

Making the Kill

Sometimes a moose backs up against a tree and refuses to budge. By standing its ground, the moose shows the pack it's ready to put up a ferocious fight. Often the wolf pack will retreat. The moose has deadly weapons—antlers and hooves—to use against the wolves.

The attack begins the second a moose starts to run.

The wolves act quickly so the moose can't escape. They move into high gear, running at 35 miles an hour. The wolves leap up to sink their fangs into soft flesh. They go for the moose's rump so they can grab onto lots of flesh without getting kicked. A brave wolf will go after the moose's nose. When a wolf locks its jaws on a moose's nose, it takes extra care to stand clear of those deadly hooves.

Once the wolves sink their teeth into their prey, they won't let go. They use every bit of strength in their mighty jaws to keep their hold. When a wolf grips onto the animal's nose, it whips its body around as hard as possible to pull the moose down. The moose tries the same tactic to shake the wolf off. When a wolf bites down on a moose's nose, the moose will thrash around and beat the wolf against the ground. Many wolves die in battle from these thrashings.

If the wolves hang on long enough, their prey will die from loss of blood or perhaps a heart attack.

Feast Now, Famine Later

The whole pack digs into the dead moose at once. They rip open its hide and tear off huge chunks of meat. In a single feeding, one wolf can eat 20 pounds of meat! That's enough meat to make eighty hamburgers.

Wolves have the perfect tools for devouring a huge moose carcass. They cut through the flesh with their fangs, crush tough bones and body parts with their molars, and scrape bones clean with their sandpaper-rough tongues.

Wolves eat just about everything: muscles, skin, fur, intestines, heart, lungs, liver, and even bones. Nothing goes to waste, not even splattered blood—if blood spills on the snow, the wolves lap it up. A favorite treat is the fat that lines the intestines.

This fat gives the wolves extra energy. The only things the animals don't eat are the leftover, chewed-up plants inside the moose's stomach.

From time to time, pack members will go down to a nearby river or lake to take a long drink. Wolves need enormous amounts of water to wash down and digest all the meat they eat. Sometimes, a wolf will sneak off by itself to bury food. First it digs a hole with its front teeth and then either drops a chunk of fresh meat or vomits half-digested meat into the hole. With its long snout, the wolf shoves mud over its food cache to conceal it. The wolf will dig up these caches when it comes back to the area later on. (Dogs bury bones for the same reason. They're saving food for later.)

After gorging for about an hour, it's time to leave the kill and take a well-deserved rest. The wolves search for a warm, open clearing. They'll even travel a few more miles to find the perfect napping ground. As soon as the pack selects a site, the wolves flop down for a long sleep. They may sleep up to 19 hours!

When the pack leaves the kill to nap, then ravens and other scavengers move in on the prey. The birds can't tear open the prey's hide, so they have to let the wolves do the carving beforehand. Only then can the birds feast.

The wolves are ready to eat more moose after their nap. They return to the carcass and finish up what the scavengers left behind. By the time the pack is through, the skull is usually the only part of the moose that's left. The feast is over.

Wolves and scavengers aren't the only living things that benefit from the death of the moose. The moose's remains disintegrate and add minerals to the soil. More plants grow in the enriched soil. More plants mean more food for rabbits, which means more rabbits survive. More rabbits mean more food for foxes, and the food chain goes on.

6

Public Enemy Number One: Humans

Not so long ago, Wisconsin was a very dangerous place for wolves. So was every other spot in North America where wolves lived. Wolves were hunted by people who felt that the animals were a threat to themselves and to their livestock. Wisconsin, like other states, paid people to kill wolves—$20 for adult wolves, $10 for pups. Over the past 150 years, the state paid millions of dollars to wipe out the wolves. Most of the money went to *wolfers*—people who hunt wolves for money. In the 1830s, 25,000 wolves lived in Wisconsin; by 1960, not a single wolf was left. It wasn't until years later that a few wolves strayed back into the state.

By 1989, thirty-five wolves lived in Wisconsin. The state no longer pays people to kill wolves; instead, concerned citizens are trying to save them. A recovery plan was designed to help the wolf population grow. But people in Wisconsin's state government knew they'd have problems with their timber wolf recovery plan. Farmers would oppose the idea

—the wolves might eat their cows and chickens. Hunters would fight the plan—saving wolves means you can't hunt them. Landowners also would oppose the plan—they worried that the wolves might attack them.

The fifth-graders from the Mead School in Wisconsin Rapids decided to help the state. They sent out a survey to people in their community to find out what people really thought about wolves.

Most people, surprisingly, wanted to save the wolf. The students sent their survey results to the state officials. Pleased with the results, the state went ahead with its recovery plan. Now wolves have a safe home in Wisconsin.

The Custer Wolf

From 1915 to 1920, thousands of wolves were slaughtered in the Dakotas and in neighboring states because of the legend of the Custer Wolf. The ranchers of Custer, South Dakota, believed that one wolf was killing many of their cattle and sheep.

The ranchers assumed that a single wolf was the mass murderer because of paw prints they found by the kills. Custer had a special distinctive mark in its paw. The ranchers offered $500 to the person who caught the Custer Wolf.

For five years, wolfers tried—and failed—to catch the Custer Wolf. Then in 1920 a man named H. P. Williams attempted the task. He had already killed the famous Split Rock Wolf in Wyoming. That wolf had supposedly killed $10,000 worth of ranch animals. If anyone could get the Custer Wolf, it was H. P. Williams. Meanwhile, wolves all over the Midwest were being killed. The only way to prove these wolves weren't Custer was to check their paws after they were dead.

It took Williams 6 months to trap the wolf. Afterward, he displayed the wolf's corpse at a ranch near the little town of Custer. One thing surprised everybody—the Custer Wolf was only a small creature. It looked like any other wolf. Williams took his $500 and moved on.

The War on Wolves

In prehistoric times, wolves and humans got along with one another. Both were social animals that wandered across the countryside. They both hunted large, hoofed animals. Eskimos knew that wolf packs could lead them to big prey, so they'd follow the wolves on hunts. (Eskimo hunters still do this today.) There was so much land and prey back then that humans and wolves didn't have to fight over food.

The trouble began when humans settled down. By cutting down forests to build farms and villages, people took away the wolf's home and hunting ground. Wolves that lived near humans couldn't find food in the depleted forests. However, there was plenty of food on the farms. Hungry wolves would go on nightly hunts to prey upon cows, chickens, and sheep. Sometimes the wolves even preyed on dogs. For protection, some people put spiked collars around their dogs' necks. The spikes could stop a wolf from biting down on a dog's throat.

Did wolves ever attack people? Only when food was extremely scarce. Most scientists believe wolves that *do* attack humans are dying from rabies, a fatal disease that makes animals very aggressive. However, in the past, people believed that *all* wolves were killers.

During the Middle Ages in Europe, wolves were called "the Devil's hounds" because they were thought to be vicious, greedy killers like the Devil himself. The body of the "evil" wolf was an important cure for "evil" illnesses: Wolf scats were used to cure eye problems; wolf paws were used to cure sore throats.

People were determined to get rid of the Devil's hounds forever. In England and Scotland, they were very successful. All the wolves in those countries were killed off about 200 years ago. When Europeans came to North America in the 1600s, they brought their families, their belongings, *and* their hatred of wolves. In a few hundred years, wolves in North America were near extinction because of people's fears.

Even as recently as 20 years ago, wolves were still hunted in great numbers. In Minnesota and Alaska, wolfers would fly small planes above wolf packs in order to shoot as many animals as possible.

In the Canadian province of British Columbia, the government decided to kill off 80 percent of the wolf population. The officials wanted to increase the number of elk, moose, and caribou, which are favorite animals of sport hunters. Thousands of wolves were shot down, poisoned with the chemical strychnine, or caught in steel-jaw traps.

The Honorable Beast

But not everyone in North America wanted the wolf dead. Many Native Americans worshiped the wolf because it was strong and courageous, and it was loyal to its family (or tribe). To peoples who lived by hunting, such as the Cree, Pawnee, and Eskimo, the wolf was revered as a wise and powerful hunter. Because these tribes lived in the same areas as wolves did, they shared their hunting grounds and had many chances to see wolves in action. These people developed a great appreciation for the wolf.

The Hidatsa Indians, who lived on the plains of North Dakota, honored the wolf for its family ties: A Hidatsa mother would rub her belly with wolf skin while giving birth to make sure she had an easy delivery. The Cheyenne honored the wolf for its intelligence: They believed that when a wolf howled, it was carrying a message from the spirit world of the dead. In tribes of the Pacific Northwest, young men performed the Whirling Wolf Dance to become an honorable member of the tribe. During the ceremony, the young men learned to act like wolves.

While most tribes praised the wolf, some shared the Europeans' fears. The Navajo, for example, thought the wolf was a witch that poisoned people and dug up dead bodies in cemeteries. The wolf witch would cut off a dead man's finger and lay it near a living person. Angry at having his finger cut off, the dead man would haunt that person forever.

Save the Wolves

If the wolfers had been successful, the wolf would have gone the way of the dinosaur and the woolly mammoth: It would have become extinct.

But what would the world be like without wolves? Hoofed animals like moose, cows, and sheep might starve to death because of overpopulation. There wouldn't be enough vegetation to feed them all. And if all the vegetation is eaten up, the habitat turns into a wasteland. By hunting sick and weak animals, wolves help keep disease from spreading among their prey. Take the wolf out of the food chain, and many living things suffer.

Before people invaded their territory, there were as many as 2 million wolves living throughout North America. Today, only 1,200 wolves live in the wild in the United States. As the number of wolves kept shrinking, people began to realize that the wolf was in real danger. That's why wolves were declared an endangered species in 1973. Now, strict laws protect these animals—anyone who shoots a wolf goes to jail.

•   •   •

Wolves, You, and the Future

If you're really interested in saving wolves, why not adopt one? Your class can become a foster parent of Sung, a wolf abandoned by her owners, or Teddy Bear, a wolf that was beaten and underfed at a roadside zoo. Both wolves were rescued by people at Wolf Haven, a nature refuge in Washington State for abused and abandoned wolves. Or how about adopting an entire wolf pack? You can adopt a pack and follow its travels through a program run by the Timber Wolf Alliance in Wisconsin.

The Timber Wolf Alliance and Wolf Haven are just two of the groups in the United States and Canada that are devoted to protecting the wolf. If you'd like to learn more about wolves, check out books about them from your local library or write to any of these groups for more information.

Get more facts. Get more involved. Make sure that wolves have a future. *You* can make a difference!

Adopt-a-Wolf Pack
Timber Wolf Alliance
Sigurd Olson
    Environmental Institute
Northland College
Ashland, WI 54806–3999

The Alaska Wildlife Alliance
P.O. Box 6953
Anchorage, AL 99502

Canadian Wolf Defenders
Box 3480, Station A
Edmonton, Alberta
Canada T5L 453

Defenders of Wildlife
1244 19th Street
Washington, D.C. 20036

HOWL (Help Our Wolves)
4600 Emerson Avenue South
Minneapolis, MN 55409

Wolf Haven America
3111 Offut Lake Road
Tenino, WA 98589
800-448-WOLF

WOLF Newsletter
P.O. Box 112
Clifton Heights, PA 19018